故園畫憶

庚寅中秋 韓磐陸題

《故园画忆系列》编委会

名誉主任：韩启德

主　　任：邵　鸿

委　　员：（按姓氏笔画为序）

　　　　　　万　捷　　王秋桂　　方李莉　　叶培贵

　　　　　　刘魁立　　况　晗　　严绍璗　　吴为山

　　　　　　范贻光　　范　芳　　孟　白　　邵　鸿

　　　　　　岳庆平　　郑培凯　　唐晓峰　　曹兵武

故园画忆系列
Memory of the Old
Home in Sketches

秘境甘南

Gannan, A Mysterious Land

贾雯婷　绘画 撰文
Sketches & Notes by Jia Wenting

学苑出版社
Academy Press

图书在版编目（CIP）数据

秘境甘南 / 贾雯婷绘画、撰文. — 北京：学苑出版社，2015.9
（故园画忆系列）
ISBN 978-7-5077-4847-5

Ⅰ.①秘… Ⅱ.①贾… Ⅲ.①速写—作品集—中国—现代 ②甘南藏族自治州—概况 Ⅳ.①J224 ②K924.22

中国版本图书馆CIP数据核字（2015）第207040号

出 版 人：	孟　白
责任编辑：	周　鼎
编　　辑：	周　扬
出版发行：	学苑出版社
社　　址：	北京市丰台区南方庄2号院1号楼
邮政编码：	100079
网　　址：	www.book001.com
电子信箱：	xueyuanpress@163.com
销售电话：	010-67601101（销售部）、67603091（总编室）
经　　销：	全国新华书店
印 刷 厂：	北京信彩瑞禾印刷厂
开本尺寸：	889×1194　1/24
印　　张：	6
字　　数：	138千字
图　　幅：	122幅
版　　次：	2015年9月北京第1版
印　　次：	2015年9月北京第1次印刷
定　　价：	42.00元

目　录

自　序　　　　　　　　　贾雯婷

宗教建筑与民居

拉卜楞寺全景	3
拉卜楞寺正门	4
拉卜楞寺贡唐宝塔和转经廊	5
拉卜楞寺大金瓦佛殿	6
拉卜楞寺德哇仓文殊佛殿	7
拉卜楞寺小金瓦寺	8
拉卜楞寺闻思学院大经堂	9
拉卜楞寺喜金刚学院	10
拉卜楞寺马头金刚圣殿	11
拉卜楞寺僧舍（一）	12
拉卜楞寺僧舍（二）	13
拉卜楞寺拜佛的信徒	14
八角城全景	15
八角城南城门	16
八角城民居	17
佐海寺经堂	18
斯柔城遗址	19
西仓寺全景	20
西仓寺寺门	21
西仓寺佛殿	22
米拉日巴佛阁外景	23
米拉日巴佛阁正门	24
郎木寺镇全景	25
郎木寺镇天葬台	26
郎木寺镇赛赤寺	27
郎木寺镇格尔底寺	28
郎木寺镇郎木寺	29
郎木寺镇挑水的僧侣	30
格尔底寺闻思殿	31
格尔底寺医学院	32
格尔底寺续部学院	33
德尔隆寺经堂	34
扎尕那全景	35
扎尕那民居	36
拉桑寺全景	37
拉桑寺正门	38
黑多村	39
录坝村	40
羊布村	41
羊布村水磨群	42
禅定寺寺门	43
禅定寺佛殿	44
贡巴寺全景	45
贡巴寺佛殿	46
贡巴寺佛塔	47
贡巴寺的朝拜者	48
贡巴寺的僧人练习法舞	49

清真寺	50	冶力关天池冶海	80
甘南民居（一）	51	冶力关阴阳石	81
甘南民居（二）	52	冶力关莲花峰	82
甘南民居（三）	53		
甘南民居（四）	54	**风俗节庆**	
临潭新城苏维埃旧址	55	玛尼石	85
俄界会议遗址	56	玛尼堆和风马旗	86
卓尼浅河上的藏桥	57	煨桑	87
藏族帐篷	58	添嘛呢箭杆的僧人	88
		磕长头（一）	89
自然造化		磕长头（二）	90
甘加草原	61	磕长头（三）	91
甘加草原上的寺庙与民居	62	寺院门前拜佛妇女	92
桑科草原	63	转转经筒的老人（一）	93
桑科草原上的牧人	64	转转经筒的老人（二）	94
桑科草原上的帐篷	65	晒佛节	95
白石崖	66	晒佛节的巨型佛像	96
白石崖溶洞	67	法舞	97
达宗湖	68	法舞面具	98
降扎温泉	69	法舞鹿神舞	99
则岔石林	70	法舞大合舞	100
则岔石林一线天	71	声乐僧	101
尕海湖	72	吹藏号的声乐僧	102
河曲马场	73	酥油花灯节（一）	103
西梅朵合塘	74	酥油花灯节（二）	104
玛曲黄河第一弯	75	酥油佛像花灯	105
骨麻湖	76	格萨尔摔跤	106
腊子口战役遗址	77	格萨尔赛马	107
大峪沟	78	赛马骑手	108
古洮州卫城遗址	79	赛牦牛	109

香浪节舞蹈	110	亮宝	120
香浪节马队表演	111	喇嘛辩经	121
博峪采花节	112	吃早饭的僧侣	122
绘制坛城的小阿卡（一）	113	献哈达	123
绘制坛城的小阿卡（二）	114	藏粑	124
绘制唐卡	115	牛背上的孩子	125
上师为弟子加持	116	甘南藏族妇女服饰	126
喇嘛向众人施与圣水	117	藏獒	127
护法僧	118	巡街仪式中的羊	128
练习法舞	119		

Contents

Preface   Jia Wenting

Religious Architecture and Residential Houses

Labrang Monastery	3
Buildings in Labrang Monastery	4
Gongtang Pagoda in Labrang Monastery	5
Dajinwa Buddhist Hall in the Labrang Monastery	6
Manjushri Buddhist Hall of Dewacang in Labrang Monastery	7
Xiaojinwa Temple in Labrang Monastery	8
Sutra Chanting Hall of Wensi Academy in Labrang Monastery	9
Hevajra Academy in Labrang Monastery	10
Sacred Hall of the Hayagriva in Labrang Monastery	11
Monk Dormitory in Labrang Monastery (1)	12
Monk Dormitory in Labrang Monastery (2)	13
A Glimpse of the Labrang Monastery	14
Octagonal City	15
South Gate Tower, the Octagonal City	16
Residential Houses in the Octagonal City	17
Zuohai Temple	18
Ruins of Ancient City Walls in Sirou City	19
Distant View of the Xicang Temple	20
A Gate of Xicang Temple	21
Buddhist Hall of Xicang Temple	22
Milarepa Buddha Pavilion	23
Main Gate of the Milarepa Buddha Pavilion	24
Town of the Langmusi	25
Zhodo Tidro Hermitage in Langmu Temple	26
Saichi Temple	27
Wensi Pavilion of the Gerdi Temple	28
Buildings of Langmu Temple	29
Monks of Langmu Temple Carrying Water	30
Flank of the Wensi Pavilion of Gerdi Temple	31
Medical School of Gerdi Temple	32
Xubu Academy and other Buildings in Gerdi Temple	33
De'erlong Temple	34
Zhagana Village	35
Residential Houses in Zhagana Village	36
Overlook View of Lasang Temple	37
Lasang Temple	38
Heiduo Village	39
Luba Village	40
Yangbu Village	41
Water Mills of the Yangbu Hill	42
Gates of the Meditation Temple	43
Buddhist Hall in the Meditation Temple	44
Panoramic View of the Gombo Temple	45
Buddhist Hall in Gombo Temple	46
Pagoda in Gombo Temple	47
A Glimpse of Gombo Temple	48
Monks of Gombo Temple Practicing	

Ceremonial Dances	49
Mosque	50
Residential Houses in Gannan (1)	51
Residential Houses in Gannan (2)	52
Residential Houses in Gannan (3)	53
Residential Houses in Gannan (4)	54
Site of the Xincheng Soviet Regime in Lintan County	55
Site of the Ejie Meeting	56
Tibetan Bridge over Zhuoniqian River	57
Tibetan Tents	58

Natural Landscape

Ganjia Grassland	61
Temples and Residential Houses on Ganjia Grassland	62
Sangke Grassland	63
Herdsmen on Sangke Grassland	64
Tents on Sangke Grassland	65
Baishi Cliff	66
Water-eroded Cave under Baishi Cliff	67
Dazong Lake	68
Jiangzha Hot Spring	69
Zecha Stone Forest	70
A Piece of Sky in Zecha Stone Forest	71
Gahai Lake	72
Horse-breeding Farm of Hequ	73
Ximeiduohe Pond	74
First Turn of the Yellow River in Maqu	75

Guma Lake	76
Site of the Lazikou Battle	77
Dayu Gorge	78
Ruins of Weicheng City of the ancient Taozhou County (now named Lintan County)	79
Alping lake Yehai of Yeliguan Town	80
Yin-yang Stones at Yeliguan Town	81
Lotus Mountain at Yeliguan Town	82

Customs and Festivals

Marnyi Stones	85
Marnyi Stone Piles and Religious Flags	86
Weisang	87
Weisang, Monks adding Mani arrow shafts	88
Long-time Kowtows (1)	89
Long-time Kowtows (2)	90
Long-time Kowtows (3)	91
Women Worshiping Buddha in Front of a Temple	92
Corridor of Prayer Wheels (1)	93
Corridor of Prayer Wheels (2)	94
Shaifo Festival	95
Huge Buddha Statue in Shaifo Festival	96
Ceremonial Dances	97
Masks of Ceremonial Dances	98
Deer-God Dancing, Ceremonial Dance	99
Mass Dancing, Ceremonial Dances	100
Music Monks	101
Monks blowing Tibetan Trombones	102
Ghee Lantern Festival (1)	103

Ghee Lantern Festival (2)	104
Buddha Statue Lantern Made of Ghee	105
Gesar Wrestling	106
Gesar Horse Racing	107
Horse Racers	108
Yak Racing	109
Dancing during Xianglang Festival	110
Horse-racing during the Xianglang Festival	111
Boyu Flower-picking Festival	112
Painting Sand Mandala (1)	113
Painting Sand Mandala (2)	114
Painting thangkas	115
A Guru Enchanting His Followers	116
Lamas Distributing Holy Water to the Public	117
Custodian Monks	118
Practicing Ceremonial Dances	119
Showing Treasures	120
Debating on Buddhist scriptures by Lamas	121
Monks Eating Breakfast	122
Presenting Khatag	123
Zangba	124
Children on the Back of Yak	125
Dresses of Tibetan Women in Gannan	126
Tibetan Mastiff	127
Sheep on Parade	128

自　序

美丽的甘南是怎样的一片天地呢？

在我看来在同一时空中起码存在着三个世界，一个是由人们衣食住行构成的世俗世界；一个是由高山、草原、湖泊构成的壮美的自然世界；还有一个就是信仰的世界。若是抽离了其中任何一项，那么呈现在您眼中的甘南都是不完整的，因为这是一片人与自然完全融合的土地。

甘南不是甘肃南部的简称，它是一个行政区——甘南藏族自治州。它位于甘肃省西南部，地处甘、青、川三省交界处，丝绸之路河南道和唐蕃道从此经过。

甘南海拔2960米，年平均气温4℃。州内有藏、汉、回、土、蒙古等24个民族，绝大多数为藏族。人们在这里过着朴素、与世无争的生活，就业压力、高额房价、拥堵的道路似乎都不存在。

但请不要认为这里是理想国。其实甘南自然条件恶劣，常年气温低，昼夜温差大；天气多变，经常风雨骤至；经济发展落后，现代化程度低，甚至有些地方依然保留着原始的生活方式。但这一切都不影响甘南成为一个富裕的精神家园。

甘南是藏传佛教的圣地，佛教寺院星罗棋布。到处有飞扬的经幡、转动的经筒和藏族人日复一日虔诚的叩拜。"世界藏学府"拉卜楞寺虽地处偏僻，却从不乏前来求学弘法的僧人。

骑着骏马在广袤草原上飞驰的汉子，是旷世英雄格萨尔王的子孙。巍峨的高山、清澈的湖水、一望无际的草原，陪伴在人们身边的牛、羊、马、狗，造就了人们宽厚、坚强的性格。这里质朴、原始，这里有令人羡慕的幸福感和满足感，这里有许多可以向世人展现的东西。

本书共收入121张甘南速写，包括宗教建筑与民居、自然风光、民俗节庆等等。我尝试用写实的手法尽量真实地展现甘南风貌，从收集资料、研究当地民俗、分配章节到绘制完成，历时一年。

在这一年中，我深受朋友、家人的鼓励和支持，每每想起真觉得情义无价，无法回报。这本书的出版，能让我用自己的绵薄之力，绘画深爱的家乡、壮美的河山，夙愿得偿。真心地感谢出版社提供的机会。

  北宋范宽喜作行旅图，在雄奇险峻的山峰下，在荒寒萧索的天地间，一行旅人困乏劳顿，艰难前行，犹如人生旅途不易。对艺术的追求之路充满艰辛，激发我不断努力。本人才学实在有限，书中尚有许多不如意之处，还望读者朋友不吝赐教。

贾雯婷

2014 年 10 月

Preface

Of what does the wonderous world Gannan consist? I think there are at least three facets: the temporal, made up of people; the natural, of mountains, grassland and lakes, all magnificent; and the one of religious beliefs. Without any one of them, Gannan cannot be fully described. Simply put, it is a place where people live in harmony with nature.

Gannan, short for Gannan Tibetan Autonomous Prefecture, is located in the southwest of the Gansu Province. Sitting at the shared border of Gansu, Qinghai and Sichuan provinces. It is of equal importance on the commercial corridors of the Henan Branch of the Silk Road and the Tang-Tibetan Old Way.

The natural environment in Gannan is severe, especially for the relatively low average temperatures year round and wide temperature variance between day and night. As the economy of the region is underdeveloped, people in some areas of Gannan still live in a primitive way.

People living in the autonomous region are mostly of Tibetan, Han, Hui, Tu and Mongolian nationalities, with Tibetan being the majority. On the vast grassland the descendants of King Gesar, a great hero in Tibet, still ride horses bravely and the people there lead a simple and peaceful life.

Known as a sacred shrine of Buddhism, Gannan is dotted with monasteries featuring religious flags and prayer wheels all around. The Lambrang Monastery in Gannan is a well known for promoting Tibetan Buddhism all over the world. Remote as it is, the monastery consistently attracts monks to come for study and to promote Buddhism. It is a spiritual world, rich with religious connotations.

The Lambrang Monastery in Gannan is well known for promoting Tibetan Buddhism all over the world. Remote as it is, the monastery consistently attracts monks to come for study and to promote Buddhism. On the vast grassland, the descendants of King Gesar , a great hero in Tibet, still ride horses bravely. It is a world surrounded by high mountains, clear lakes and endless grassland occupied by cows, sheep, horses and dogs. The people there are kind and strong-minded. On this land of wonder, people can find simplicity, beauty, happiness and the satisfaction for which they are eager.

In this book there are 121 sketches of Gannan, depicting religious buildings, residential houses, natural scenery, folklore and festive celebrations as subjects. When working on these paintings, I adopted a realistic method of portrayal in order to showcase the authentic features of Gannan. It took me a year to complete, gathering materials, researching the folklore, chapter planning and, finally, painting.

The publishing of this book is the realization of a long-cherished dream of mine, to sketch out and share the magnificent landscape of my beloved hometown.

I'd like to take this opportunity to express my gratitude to my families and friends for all the encouragement and support they have given to me this past year.

Jia Wenting
October, 2014

宗教建筑与民居
Religious Architecture and Residential Houses

拉卜楞寺全景

位于甘南藏族自治州夏河县城西 500 米处，藏语全称为噶丹夏珠达尔吉扎西益苏奇具琅，旧称扎西奇寺，一般称为拉卜楞寺。它是藏传佛教格鲁派六大寺院之一，被誉为"世界藏学府"。

Labrang Monastery

500 meters west of Xiahe County, it is also known as Zhaqixi Monastery. As one of the six major monasteries of the Gelug School of Tibetan Buddhism, it is praised as an international institution for the promotion of Tibetan Buddhism.

拉卜楞寺正门

　　拉卜楞寺于清康熙四十八年（1709年）建寺，在280余年间，这些由红墙、白墙、金顶构成的建筑形成了特点明显的藏族寺院建筑群。

Buildings in Labrang Monastery
Built in 1709, the 48th year since Emperor Kangxi (1662-1722) took the reign of the Qing Dynasty (1644-1911). In the years that followed more houses were built, making this monastery an architectural compound with distinctive features of Tibet.

拉卜楞寺贡唐宝塔和转经廊

贡唐宝塔位于拉卜楞寺西南角，因贡唐仓院而得名。宝塔外形金碧辉煌，内部构造精巧，塔高五层，由塔刹、塔瓶、塔座三部分组成。塔外就是拉卜楞寺著名的转经廊，长3000米，有1700多个转经筒，能环绕寺庙二分之一。

Gongtang Pagoda in Labrang Monastery

Located at the Gongtangcang Temple in the southwest of Labrang Monastery, this is a five-storied pagoda with a corridor of prayer wheels outside.

拉卜楞寺大金瓦佛殿

大金瓦佛殿，又称弥勒佛殿。该殿为藏汉混合式结构，最高层为宫殿式的方亭，四角飞檐，其上有鎏金铜狮、铜龙、铜宝瓶、铜法轮、铜如意，阳光下金碧辉煌，故称"大金瓦寺"。

Dajinwa Buddhist Hall in the Labrang Monastery

Also known as the Buddhist Hall of Maitreya, it is a shining building combining the architectural style of both Han and Tibetan nationalities. The top story is a palatial pavilion with four sides.

拉卜楞寺德哇仓文殊佛殿

德哇仓文殊佛殿，巍然耸立于拉卜楞寺正南，面临大夏河，背倚拉卜楞寺大经堂。佛殿高四层，其外观为石墙、柽柳墙建筑结构。以藏式石木为主，外石内木，外不见木、内不见石，整洁大方，坚固耐久。

Manjushri Buddhist Hall of Dewacang in Labrang Monastery
Located in the south of Labrang Monastery. The hall faces the Daxia River and is backed by the Sutra Chanting Hall of Labrang Monastery. It is a four-storey Tibetan-style building constructed of wood and timber.

拉卜楞寺小金瓦寺

　　拉卜楞寺释迦牟尼殿，俗称"小金瓦寺"，位于弥勒殿西侧，仿拉萨大昭寺修建，亦为鎏金铜瓦屋顶。

Xiaojinwa Temple in Labrang Monastery
Located in the west of the Maitreya Hall, it was built in style of the Jokhang Temple and is commonly known as the Xiaojinwa Temple which literally means "small golden tile temple."

拉卜楞寺闻思学院大经堂

拉卜楞寺共有六大经堂,其中最大的是闻思学院经堂,又称大经堂。经堂内有140根巨大的柱子,可同时容纳1200名学僧上课,是全寺之中枢。

Sutra Chanting Hall of Wensi Academy in Labrang Monastery

As the biggest among the six halls for chanting sutra in Labrang Monastery, it is also known as the Main Assembly Hall for Sutra Chanting. There are 140 huge pillars and it is able to accommodate 1,200 people.

> 拉卜楞寺喜金刚学院

喜金刚学院主要研究喜金刚的生起和圆满次第之道，兼习音乐、韵律、法舞等，可以说是藏传佛教的艺术学院。

Hevajra Academy in Labrang Monastery

An artistic academy of Tibetan Buddhism famous for its research on the kye-rim and dzog-rim of Hevajra. It is also a place for studying music, rhythm and ceremonial dances.

拉卜楞寺马头金刚圣殿

殿内供奉的马头明王是观世音菩萨的愤怒相,传说可以帮助修行者祛除魔障。马头明王塑像高 12 米,铜质鎏金,高大壮观。

Sacred Hall of the Hayagriva in Labrang Monastery

There is a 12-meter statue of the Avalokitesvara consecrated in the hall. In Tibetan Buddhism, Avalokitesvara is a Buddha believed to be a protector of practitioners from demons.

拉卜楞寺僧舍（一）

僧舍也是拉卜楞寺建筑群的主要组成部分，是一般僧侣居住的地方，为土木结构的平顶房，每院可居住三四人。

Monk Dormitory in Labrang Monastery (1)

A dormitory courtyard in the monastery accommodates three to four monks. It consists of rooms of flat roofs and is constructed of earth and wood.

拉卜楞寺僧舍（二）

拉卜楞寺有近千间僧舍，占地1000多亩，构成大大小小、鳞次栉比的院落。其中有些院落是汉式建筑，采用硬山瓦顶，有许多砖雕和汉式彩画。

Monk Dormitory in Labrang Monastery (2)

There are about a thousand monk dormitories covering an area of over 1,000 mu (15mu=1 hectare). Some of them are Han-style architecture, decorated with carved brickwork and Han-style colored paintings.

拉卜楞寺拜佛的信徒

在拉卜楞寺随处都可见到虔诚拜佛的信徒，他们背负行囊，从千里之外赶来，一步一磕头，初衷不改。这是一个由信仰构成的佛国世界。

A Glimpse of the Labrang Monastery

It is completely natural to meet with devout followers of Buddhism in the sacred monastery.

八角城全景

　　八角城建于秦汉时期，位于甘加草原的东部，曾经是古代的军事要塞，距今有2000多年的历史。八角城因其有八个城角而得名，城郭是一个空心的十字形。

Octagonal City

Built in the Qin (221BC-206BC) or Han (202BC-220AD) Dynasties, the ancient city was once a military post. It boasts a history of over 2,000 years.

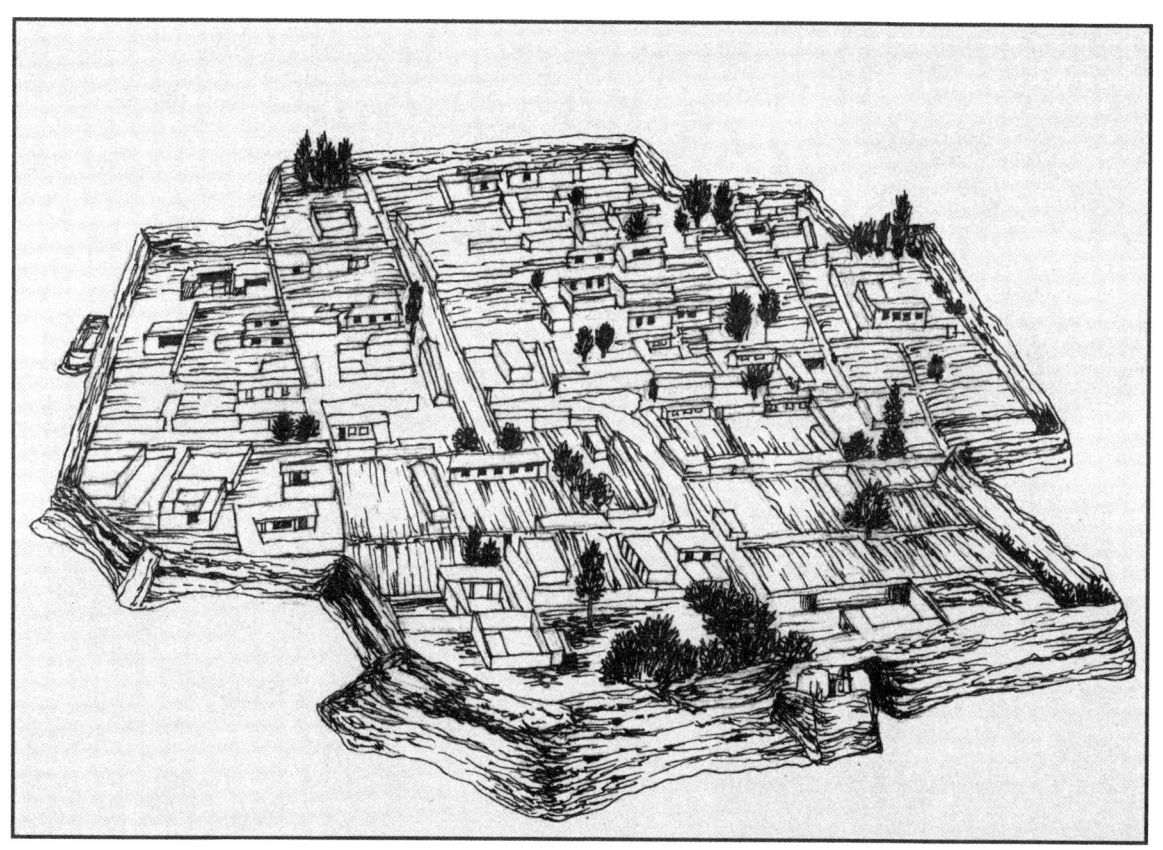

八角城南城门

南城门墙基厚 1.4 米，高 13.5 米，顶宽 5.2 米。门前两端较为开阔，是当年八角城的唯一通道。

South Gate Tower, the Octagonal City

The part of the wall linking with the gate 13.5 meters high and 5.2 meters wide at the top with a base height of 1.4 meters. The gate was once the only channel to the Octagonal City with spacious and open areas on both sides.

八角城民居

　　八角城民居为土木结构，平顶，至今还有人居住。居民们每天会派一人在城门口收取参观费。

Residential Houses in the Octagonal City

These are houses constructed of earth and wood with flat roofs. They are still inhabited to this day.

佐海寺经堂

位于夏河县东北方风光秀美的大象山之下。它是甘南藏区历史最悠久的藏传佛教寺院之一，也是甘南唯一一座藏族原始宗教寺庙。

Zuohai Temple

Located at the northeast of Xiahe County, it is the oldest temple of Tibetan Buddhism in the Tibetan area of Gannan. It is also known as the only temple of the primitive Tibetan religion in Gannan.

斯柔城遗址

位于甘加滩央曲河与恰莫控曲河汇合的西北台地上,这块台地是25度的斜坡,前低后高。古城内原来的建筑依稀可辨,大殿、前殿、偏殿、后殿、回廊,鳞次栉比,对称美观。

Ruins of Ancient City Walls in Sirou City

Located on the valley terrace, original buildings of the ancient city are vaguely discernible. The main hall, front hall, side hall, back hall and corridors lay, symmetrically, row upon row and are still popular tourist destinations.

西仓寺全景

位于碌曲县东十千米处，是较为著名的格鲁派寺院之一。该寺坐北朝南，背靠形似银灰色卧象的山莽，滚滚洮河水绕寺而过，自西向东流。寺院周围苍松翠柏，四季常青，呈现出一派静谧祥和之态。

Distant View of the Xicang Temple

Facing south, the temple is 10 kilometers east of Luqu County, it is surrounded by verdant pines and cypress trees that remain green all year round.

> 西仓寺寺门

　　西仓寺是在当地原有的几座小寺的基础上建立起来的，始建于清道光十九年（1839年），由拉卜楞寺著名高僧第三世德哇仓·嘉央图丹尼玛主持建造。

A Gate of Xicang Temple

Built in 1839 by merging several smaller temples, its construction was led by an eminent monk from the Labrang Monastery.

西仓寺佛殿

西仓寺宏大庄严的建筑在20世纪六七十年代遭到严重毁坏。1982年该寺逐步得以恢复，重建了大经堂和护法殿，设立了闻思学院，僧众达150余人。

Buddhist Hall of Xicang Temple

It suffered from severe damage in history. After 1982, the Sutra Enchanting Hall and the Dharmapalas Hall (Dharmapalas, literally means "preserving the dharma") were rebuilt and the Wensi Academy was established. Now there are more than 150 monks in the temple.

米拉日巴佛阁外景

　　被当地人称为九层楼，始建于清乾隆四十二年（1777年）。原建筑已遭到损坏，现在的建筑是1992年重新修建的。佛阁内有反映藏传佛教内容的巨大壁画，技法高超，笔法娴熟，具有很高的艺术价值。

Milarepa Buddha Pavilion

First built in 1777, it was known locally as the Nine-Floor Temple. The pavilion left was rebuilt in 1992.

| 米拉日巴佛阁正门 |

位于甘肃安多藏区合作市，全称是"安多合作米拉日巴九层佛阁"。为纪念米拉日巴而修建，是藏传佛教噶举派（白教）在安多藏区最主要的寺院。

Main Gate of the Milarepa Buddha Pavilion

Located at Hezuo City of the Amdo and occupied by many Tibetans, the Milarepa Buddha Pavilion is the most important temple of the Kagyu School (white school) of Tibetan Buddhism in the Amdo.

郎木寺镇全景

横跨甘肃、四川两省，以白龙江为界。白龙江的西北一侧属于甘肃省管辖，白龙江的东南一侧属于四川省管辖。镇上常住人口有 3000 多人，居民以藏族为主，杂居着一些汉族和回族。

Town of the Langmusi
Sitting on the border of Gansu and Sichuan Provinces, the town is surrounded by mountains and mainly inhabited by Tibetans.

郎木寺镇天葬台

位于赛赤寺西北300多米处，是安多地区最大的天葬台之一，已有400多年的历史。藏传佛教认为，人的身体由水、火、土、风四种元素构成，人死以后应该将身体以合适的形式归还给自然，所以有水葬、火葬、土葬和天葬。天葬仪式务必请大家不要观看，要尊重当地风俗习惯，祝死者顺利往生。

Zhodo Tidro Hermitage in Langmu Temple

It is the biggest Zhodo Tidro Hermitage in the Amdo and with a 400 year history. According to Tibetan Buddhism, the human body is composed of four basic elements, water, fire, earth and wind. They believe that the human body after death should be returned to the nature in a suitable way, though four distinct burial forms, water burial, cremation, inhumation and sky burial (or Zhodo Tidro Hermitage).

> 郎木寺镇赛赤寺

　　"赛赤"为藏文音译，有"金色的宝座"之意。赛赤寺的第一世活佛降参桑格聪慧过人、德行高超，在西藏求学期间获得了佛学界授予的最高学位和荣誉——赤哇，俗称"赛赤"。

Saichi Temple

With the name meaning of "the golden throne", the temple is quite famous in the Amdo. Its founder, Jiangshen Sange, was awarded the highest academic degree and honor in Buddhism, the Chiwa, which means "abbot of a temple."

郎木寺镇格尔底寺

白龙江从郎木寺镇中穿过，江北是赛赤寺，江南是格尔底寺。格尔底寺由黄派创始人宗喀巴大师的弟子，第一世格尔登活佛于明永乐十一年（1413年）初建，以后逐步形成续部、闻思、时轮、藏医、刻经等五大学院。

Wensi Pavilion of the Gerdi Temple
The Bailong River runs through the Town of Langmusi with Saichi Temple on the north bank and Gerdi Temple on the south.

郎木寺镇郎木寺

随着旅游业的发展，郎木寺一带到处都在翻盖房屋、修整马路，成为甘南地区变化最快的地方。

Buildings of Langmu Temple

Thanks to the development of tourism, old houses and roads have been restored and new ones built making this the temple with the most changes in Gannan.

郎木寺镇挑水的僧侣

在郎木寺镇,僧侣和百姓住在一起,修行者八岁时授沙弥戒,即可进入寺院修行。21岁授比丘戒,正式成为一名出家人。其中,年轻的僧人大多会讲简单的汉语和英语。

Monks of Langmu Temple Carrying Water

In the town of Langmusi, monks live together with ordinary citizens. Practitioners were sent to temples when they were 8 years old and may officially become monks at 21 years old. Most young monks at Langmu Temple can speak some Chinese and even English.

格尔底寺闻思殿

格尔底寺全称"达仓纳摩格尔底寺院",系四川阿坝地区格鲁派规模最大、最具影响力的寺院之一,辖有18座分寺,现有僧人500多人。图为格尔底寺闻思殿。

Flank of the Wensi Pavilion of Gerdi Temple

As the biggest and most influential temple of the Gelug School of Tibetan Buddhism, Gerdi temple administrates 18 affiliated temples and houses more than 500 monks.

> 格尔底寺医学院

格尔底寺包括闻思殿、医学院、时轮殿和护法殿，寺庙里建有佛学院，相当于小学、初中阶段的佛教教育。图为医学院建筑。

Medical School of Gerdi Temple

The Gerdi Temple is composed of Wensi Hall, a medical school, a Shilun hall, Dharmapalas Hall and a Buddhism academy, which provides Buddhist education at primary and secondary levels.

格尔底寺续部学院

　　格尔底寺是所有藏传佛教寺院中唯一拥有活佛肉身的寺院，而其他藏传佛教寺院都只有佛骨舍利。图为格尔底寺续部学院。

Xubu Academy and other Buildings in Gerdi Temple

Among all Tibetan Buddhist temples, only the Gerdi Temple has the body of a rinpoche while others only preserve sharipu, which is ash of rinpoche.

德尔隆寺经堂

全称为"德尔隆益嘎曲僧林",也称沙沟寺,位于夏河县王格尔塘乡西南约5000米处。该寺因所在山谷名称而得名,意为"宝藏谷"。图为德尔隆寺的经堂。

De'erlong Temple

It is 5,000 meters southwest to the Wangge'ertang Township of Xiahe County. The De'erlong Valley where the temple sits means "the valley of treasure", and the temple derives its name from the valley.

扎尕那全景

藏语扎尕那，即石头城。距离迭部县城 28 千米，曾经是洮迭古道（临潭到迭部）上的一个重要驿站。随着古道荒废，藏族村寨也回归原生态。村子四周包围着壮观的石壁，像一座巨型的石头宫殿。

Zhagana Village

28 kilometers from the Diebu County seat, the village was an important courtier station on the Ancient Taodie- Diebu Road for centuries. Encircled by lofty walls, the village resembles a giant stone palace.

扎尕那民居

　　这里的民居大都为传统的踏板房，木制为主，有很强的地方特色，甘南迭部县一带也有这种民宅。

Residential Houses in Zhagana Village

Most families in Zhagana village live in the houses with footboards on the roofs. These wooden houses are quite often seen around Diebu County of Sichuan Province.

拉桑寺全景

　　拉桑寺是当地信教群众进行宗教活动的主要场所，它与民居相融合，使人越发感到佛法就在平淡生活中。

Overlook View of Lasang Temple

The Lasang Temple is an integral place for local believers to worship. As an integral part of the local residential building complex, it inspires people to feel the existence of dharma in everyday life.

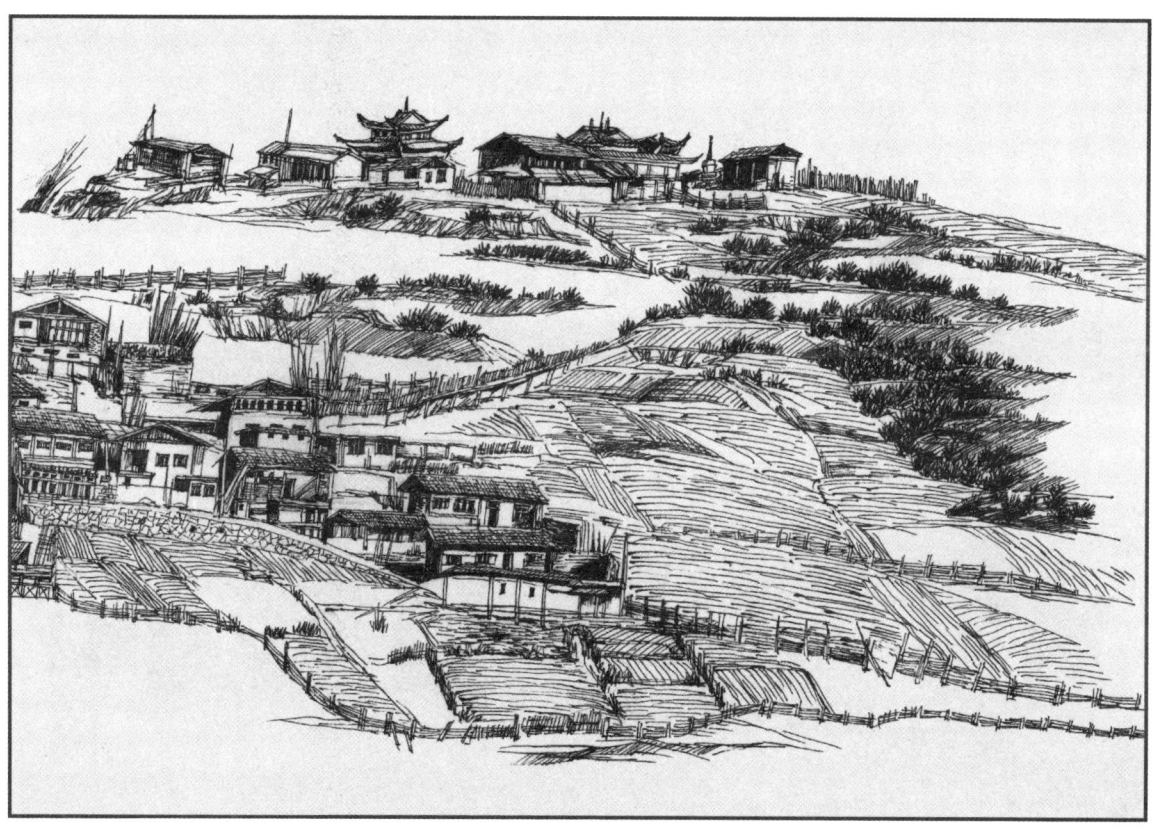

拉桑寺正门

　　拉桑寺始建于清顺治二年（1645年），现有经堂二座，僧舍30余间，住寺僧侣40余人。信教群众来自周边7个自然村，约2500余人。图为拉桑寺正门。

Lasang Temple
Built in 1645 the temple now sports two sutra chanting rooms and roughly 30 dormitories. It is home to more than 40 monks, and allows 2500 believers of the 7 natural villages to pay homage within its walls regularly.

位于甘南藏族自治州迭部县腊子口乡，共有村民 139 户，是典型的藏族小山村。

Heiduo Village

Located in the Lazikou Town of Diebu County in the Gannan Gansu Province, this is a typical Tibetan village with 139 households.

录坝村

位于迭部县洛大乡，是一个只有 40 户居民的藏族小山村，村民们一直过着简朴平静的生活。

Luba Village

A small Tibetan village with 40 households in the Luoda Town, Diebu County. Life there has always been simple and serene.

> 羊布村

　　它是坐落在高山坡顶上的一个很大的藏寨，三面环山，一面临江，整个寨子仿佛挂在天边。

Yangbu Village

It is a large, traditional Tibetan village near the top of a high mountain. Surrounded by mountains on three sides and with a river running through it, the village appears to be hanging on the sky.

羊布村水磨群

　　进入四川之前翻越的最后一道山梁叫羊布梁,山高水急,河道落差较大。在长度不足 150 米的河段上,你会看到 11 个水磨坊横跨在水面上,这就是著名的羊布水磨群。

Water Mills of the Yangbu Hill

The last mountain before entering Sichuan Province from Gansu is named Yangbu Hill. On a river not far from the hill, there are 11 water mills along the river reach of less than 150 meters. That is the famous Yangbu Water Mills.

> 禅定寺寺门

　　禅定寺位于甘南卓尼县城西北的台地上,是甘南历史上最悠久的藏传佛教寺庙,一度曾是川、甘、藏区三大佛教寺院之一,鼎盛时期有寺僧5000多人。

Gates of the Meditation Temple

The Meditation Temple is the most time-honored among all monasteries and temples in Gannan. Hosting more than 5000 monks at its active peak, it has been ranked several times among the top three Buddhist temples in the Tibetan regions of Gansu and Qinghai.

▎禅定寺佛殿

　　现存禅定寺的建筑是 20 世纪 80 年代以来整体重修的，包括大经堂、密宗学院、时轮学院等 80 多座建筑。佛殿庄严肃穆，巍然屹立。

Buddhist Hall in the Meditation Temple
Buildings in the temple have undergone a thorough overhaul after the 1980s. Today it stands firm and solemn.

贡巴寺全景

贡巴寺位于贵德县城东南 3000 米处的小泉山下，即河东乡贡巴村东侧。由许多殿宇、经堂、佛塔、僧舍组成，其建筑具有汉、藏两种风格，是贵德地区颇负盛名的佛教圣地。

Panoramic View of the Gombo Temple

Located under the Xiaoquan Mountain, 3 kilometers southeast to the Gui'de County and combining the building style of Han and Tibetan nationalities, the temple has long been held as sacred land in the county.

贡巴寺佛殿

贡巴寺始建于清光绪十四年（1888年），整体建筑金碧辉煌，僧人住的禅房规制整齐，看起来庄严肃穆。

Buddhist Hall in Gombo Temple

These magnificent buildings were built in 1888. The solemn meditation rooms where monks live are of the same size and styles.

> 贡巴寺佛塔

　　位于寺院最北端，几乎是拉卜楞寺贡唐宝塔的翻版，华丽无比。

Pagoda in Gombo Temple

Located at the north end of the temple, the pagoda is a gorgeous rival to the Gongtang Pagoda of the Labrang Monastery.

贡巴寺的朝拜者

贡巴寺院内放置着经筒和刻有经文的牦牛头骨，虔诚的信仰者在朝拜祈祷。

A Glimpse of Gombo Temple

Prayer wheels and yak skulls inscribed with scriptures are placed throughout the temple. Devout believers come to worship and pray for blessing.

贡巴寺的僧人练习法舞

贡巴寺设有专业性的法舞学院,学法舞的僧人不仅要苦练舞蹈动作,还要学习密宗咒语和坐禅修行。

Monks of Gombo Temple Practicing Ceremonial Dances

There is a specialized academy teaching ceremonial dances in the temple. Monks learn not only steps and movements of the dancing, but also the Tantric mantra and meditation practices.

清真寺

清真寺位于格尔底寺不远处,其建筑样式是典型的伊斯兰风格,但细节处带有一些藏式特色的痕迹。

Mosque

This is a mosque not far from the Gerdi Temple. It is a building with typical Islamic style with some Tibetan features to be found in its details.

甘南民居（一）

甘南民居一般都是平顶立体四合院式的房屋，分为灶房、卧室、佛堂、畜圈、贮藏室、柴廊、草房、厕所等八处。院墙高三四米，底宽一米左右。

Residential Houses in Gannan (1)

Most residential house compounds in Gannan are quadrangle courtyards composed of houses with flat roofs and differentiated heights. The houses usually consist of eight functional units: a kitchen, bedrooms, a Buddhist hall, a corral, a storage room, a firewood corridor, a haystack room and a toilet. The wall of the yard is about 3-4 meters high and 1 meter thick at the base.

甘南民居（二）

　　农历十月的草原开始封冻，牧民结束游牧生活，返回定居的冬帐房。冬帐房是用木料搭成矮小屋架后，四壁糊上牛粪，屋顶用泥土填平，使之不透风，矮小狭窄，形如窑洞。因制造简陋，每年都须修补。

Residential Houses in Gannan (2)

When the prairies enter rest grazing period during the cold month of October in the lunar calendar, the nomadic life also ends and herdsmen return and settle down in winter tents. The frames of these tents are basically made of wood. Walls are pasted with cow dung, and the roofs with earth to make it airtight for protection against the frigid prairie winds.

甘南民居（三）

碉房是最常见的藏族民居建筑形式，它是一种用石头垒砌或土筑而成的房屋，高三四层。因外观很像碉堡，故称为碉房。

Residential Houses in Gannan (3)

Blockhouses are the most common residential buildings of Tibetans. They are 3-4 story houses built by piling up of stones and/or earth. Because of the appearance resembling those of pillboxes, they are often referred to as blockhouses.

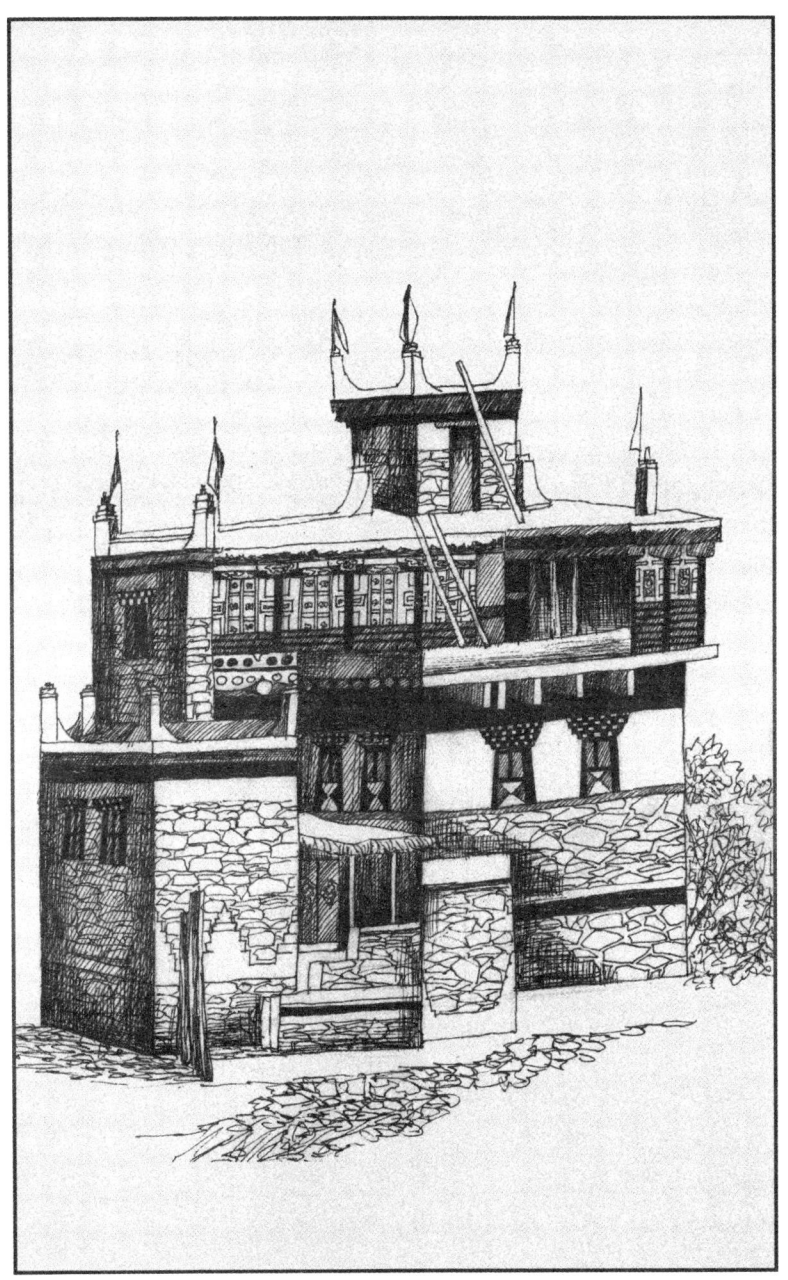

甘南民居（四）

藏族是善于表现美的民族，对于居所的装饰十分讲究。一般民居或是在门上绘制日月祥云图，或是悬挂风马旗。门套窗套渲染成黑色，极具装饰性，更是藏族民居最醒目的标识。

Residential Houses in Gannan (4)

Decorations of Tibetan houses are quite exquisite. Residential buildings there often feature doors decorated with the paintings of sun, moon and auspicious clouds, or hung with religious flags. Frames of doors and windows are usually painted black. These features, among others, make Tibetan houses into decorative artworks.

临潭新城苏维埃旧址

位于明代洮州卫城之内，旧称鞑王金銮殿，始建于元代（1271～1368年）。它不仅是一处具有800年历史的古迹景观，还是近代革命圣地。

Site of the Xincheng Soviet Regime in Lintan County

The county was founded in the 13th century of the Ming Dynasty (1368-1644) and is a key cultural relic protection unit in Gansu Province. It has an historic landscape dating back 800 years as well as sites of the revolution during modern times.

俄界会议遗址

位于甘肃省迭部县东南 68 千米处的达拉乡高吉村。俄界会议是红军长征途中开的一次重要会议，它对于胜利完成"两万五千里长征"具有极其重要的意义。

Site of the Ejie Meeting

Located in the Gaoji Village of Dala Town and 68 kilometers southeast to Diebu County, the Ejie Meeting, took place on Sep12th, 1935 during the Long March of the Red Army. It is a significant event in the completion of the Long March.

卓尼浅河上的藏桥

在甘南藏区经常可以看到这种由原木搭制而成的桥梁，就地取材、朴实耐用。

Tibetan Bridge over Zhuoniqian River

This type of wooden bridge is commonly found in the Tibetan area of Gannan. Made of timber from local forests, these bridges are simple but sturdy.

藏族帐篷

帐篷是牧民流动的家，是藏族牧区人民的主要住房样式。有一种帐篷是用牦牛毛加工而成的，为黑色，结实耐用；还有一种是白布帐篷，周围镶上黑色、蓝色或棕色的布边，里面加一层有色布料，外面印带有宗教色彩的图案。白色帐篷过去多见于寺院或举行宗教仪式的场所，现在甘南藏区处处可见。

Tibetan Tents

For Tibetan herdsmen, tents are the major housing style. There are mainly two types, one processed from yak fur, and the other made of white cloth. In the past, tents were more common in temples or other arenas for religious ceremonies. Nowadays, they function more as a family necessity.

自然造化
Natural Landscape

> **甘加草原**

位于夏河县城西北 20 千米处，周围群山环绕，是一处典型的高原草地，牧草肥沃，是理想的天然牧场。每到夏季，整个草原碧绿如茵，好似一块天然的绿色大地毯。拉卜楞寺的创建者第一世嘉木样活佛就诞生在这里。

Ganjia Grassland

20 kilometers northwest of Xiahe County, mountains surround the grassland. It is typical plateau grassland. Every summer, the grassland turns into a beautiful piece of natural green carpet. It was the birthplace of Master Jamyang I, the founder of the Labrang Monastery.

甘加草原上的寺庙与民居

甘加草原四周群山环绕，点点民居散落在山脚下。有居民的地方就有寺庙，寺庙与民居相依相伴，共同构成人们生活和精神的和谐家园。

Temples and Residential Houses on Ganjia Grassland

Mountains encircle the grassland. Residential houses are scattered around at the foot of mountains. Temples and residential houses together constitute the harmonious home of physical and spiritual life of the people.

> 桑科草原

　　位于甘南藏族自治州夏河境内，属于草甸草原，面积达 70 平方千米，平均海拔在 3000 米以上。这里是当地牧民的冬季牧场，夏天只有风吹草低，却不见牛羊。

Sangke Grassland

In Xiahe County of Gannan Tibetan Autonomous Prefecture in Gansu Province. This is a meadow steppe at an average attitude of approximately 3000 meters.

桑科草原上的牧人

　　桑科草原上的牧人长期在外游牧，只有冬季会回到这里放牧，他们拥有豪爽朴实的性格。

Herdsmen on Sangke Grassland

They move about in search of pasture for most times during the year only to return to the Sangke Grassland in winter. They are typical herdsmen, simple and straightforward.

桑科草原上的帐篷

在一望无际的桑科草原上散落着一顶顶美丽的帐篷，它们是牧民在草原上流动的家。

Tents on Sangke Grassland

Beautiful tents on the endless grassland are portable homes for the itinerant herdsman.

白石崖

　　距离夏河约 50 千米的白石崖，是当地人眼中的神圣之地。偌大的草原齐齐地被裁割下来，分成上、下两层，层与层之间形成了一道很长很高的陡峭石崖，当地人称"白石崖"。从远处望，石崖恰似白玉屏风横在半空，在蓝天碧日辉映下熠熠闪光，蔚为壮观。

Baishi Cliff

50 kilometers away from Xiahe County, local people see it as a sacred place. It cuts the grassland into two layers, making a magnificent view under the blue sky on the grassland.

白石崖溶洞

在白石崖根部偏西处，有一眼可容三四人进出的溶洞，洞里有潺潺流水，曲径通幽，熔岩造型千姿百态、惟妙惟肖。

Water-eroded Cave under Baishi Cliff

Close to the west end of the cliff bottom there is a water-eroded cave with a width for three to four people to pass at one time. Inside the cave there are gurgling streams and lava rocks of various shapes and sizes.

达宗湖

为不规则葫芦形的高山堰塞湖,平日湖边少有人迹,隐约能看到几只飘扬在冽冽寒风中的经幡。

Dazong Lake

A dammed, gourd-shaped mountain lake. It is, for the most part, rarely visited and religious flags flutter in the wind.

降扎温泉

距离郎木寺大约30千米,在几处泉眼上依山势修建了具有藏族和汉族特色的半遮蔽式凉亭,泉水水温高达51度,含有丰富的硫磺铁等矿物质,人们相信它可以治疗关节炎、皮肤病。降扎温泉在川、甘、藏地区有很高的知名度,历来有"神圣吉祥"之地的美称。

Jiangzha Hot Spring

Approximately 30 meters away from Langmu Temple, above some of the springs with preferable topographic conditions, semi-closed pavilions were built. These are buildings with Han and Tibetan features. Among Tibetans in Sichuan, Gansu and Qinhai provinces, the spring enjoys great notoriety and is always seen as a sacred and auspicious place.

则查石林

　　由地壳上升形成的硅灰石景观，全长 10 千米。它经过长年累月的风雨剥蚀，形成形状怪异的奇峰异石，远远望去犹如一片岩石森林。

Zecha Stone Forest
A landscape of siliceous limestone formed after the movements of the earth's crust. It was located at an area of approximately 10 kilometers long. Huge stones in peculiar shapes were formed over many years of erosion by wind and rain. From afar these stones appear like a forest, which is how it derives its name.

【则岔石林一线天】

壁立千仞的石峰间有长近百米的"石门一线天",宽仅容一驮畜经过,潺潺流水穿石门而过。石门内修有百米长的木栈道,有"一夫当关、万夫莫开"之险,是进入石林的必经之路。

A Piece of Sky in Zecha Stone Forest

This is a piece of sky among huge and precipitous rock approximately one hundred meters long. The passage is so narrow that it is quite difficult for even cattle to pass. Inside the path, there is a wooden plank road stretching over one hundred meters. It leads tourists in and out as their only passage to the stone forest.

尕海湖

"尕"就是"小"的意思，尕海湖就是像小海一样的湖。它是甘南第一大淡水湖，也是青藏高原东部一块重要湿地，被誉为"高原小珍珠"。

Gahai Lake

Ga, is a character meaning "small" in the local dialect. As suggested by the name, Gahai Lake is like a small sea. It is the largest fresh water lake in Gannan and is surrounded by the wetland crucial for eastern regions of the Qinghai-Tibet Plateau. It has been praised as the Pearl on the Plateau.

> 河曲马场

位于玛曲县城东南20千米处的乔科草原东北部,包括万涎滩、文保滩、乔科滩,有"河曲水浒"之称。这里是河曲马的培育中心,据说格萨尔王16岁时在河曲找到了马中之王——赤兔马。河曲马场以培育良马而闻名,这里每年都会举办赛马大会。

Horse-breeding Farm of Hequ

Located in the northeast of Qiaoke Steppe, some 20 kilometers southeast of Maqu County. The farm is a breeding center of Hequ horses. Famous for the quality of horses it breeds, the farm is also host to the grand annual racing games.

西梅朵合塘

意为"吉祥花滩",位于玛曲县城以西 120 千米处的欧拉秀玛乡。每年 7、8、10 月几乎都有不同的花海展现,尤其是 10 月,在严寒中盛开的毛茛花十分美丽。

Ximeiduohe Pond

Meaning "the auspicious beach of flowers", it is located in Eulerxiuma County approximately 120 kilometers away from Maqu County. A great number of flowers are on display each year in July, August and October. The sea of ranunculus asiaticus during the chilly month of October is especially beautiful.

> 玛曲黄河第一弯

　　从巴颜喀拉山发源的黄河一路东行，在玛曲县形成了总长度达 433 千米的一个 180 度大转弯，被称为黄河"首曲"。

First Turn of the Yellow River in Maqu

Originating in the Bayan Har Mountains in Qinghai Province in western China, the Yellow River flows east until it reaches Maqu, where it takes a 180-degree turn of approximately 433 kilometers. This segment in Maqu came to be known as "The First Turn of the Yellow River."

骨麻湖

又称为"玉湖",位于迭部县桑坝乡黑拉村西北部的半山腰。湖面呈椭圆形,湖水的背景是高耸的迭山山脉,山头积雪终年不化。"迭山横雪"也是一道永恒的风景。

Guma Lake

Also known as the "Jade Lake", it has an oval surface. With the towering Dieshan Mountains as the backdrop, the scenery of the lake is breathtaking beneath the snow-capped peaks.

腊子口战役遗址

位于甘肃省迭部县东北部的腊子乡。1935年9月红军因地制宜，采用包抄战术，打开了中央红军北上进入陕甘的通道。

Site of the Lazikou Battle

Located in Lazi Town northeast of Diebu County, this site saw the Red Army adjust its fighting strategy to local conditions in September of 1935 and outflank its rivals, clearing the way to Shanxi and Gansu provinces.

> 大峪沟

　　位于甘南卓居县木耳乡，全长 81 千米，河流曲折有致，澄碧甘甜。流域内处处可见鱼翔浅底、麝鹿啜饮，真是妙趣横生、自然天成。

Dayu Gorge

Located in Mu'er Town of Gannan, the gorge is approximately 81 kilometers long. With the Dayu River winding through, it is rich in wildlife resources making it a lively and enjoyable tourist destination.

古洮州卫城遗址

　　这座甘南地区最大的古城是明洪武十二年（1379年）西平侯沐英所筑。该城依山而建，东北高西南低，呈多边形，周长约5000多米。

Ruins of Weicheng City of the ancient Taozhou County (now named Lintan County)

The ancient town was built in 1379. It was built at the foot of the mountains and the elevation is higher at the northeast and lower at the southwest. It is shaped like a polygon with a circumference of over 5000 meters.

> 冶力关天池冶海

位于甘南临潭县境内以北 7000 米处的白石山与庙花山之间，是一个高峡平湖。冶海是天然淡水湖，池东石崖和白石山相对矗立，池水青中泛绿，山峦树木倒映池中，山水云天浑然一体，随波摇曳，景色异常壮观。

Alping lake Yehai of Yeliguan Town

A freshwater alpine lake formed between the Baishi Mountain and the Miaohua Mountain, this is approximately 7000 meters north of the Yeliguan Pass. With the inverted reflection of mountains and forests in the turquoise water, the scenery is both unique and magnificent.

冶力关阴阳石

位于甘南临潭县冶力关镇西南约 2000 米处，因其形状酷似雌雄阴阳之物而得名。阴阳石四周群山环绕，绿树成荫。

Yin-yang Stones at Yeliguan Town

It was also named "divine stones of Ci and Xiong" (meaning female and male respectively in Chinese). It is approximately 2000 meters southwest of Yeliguan Town. Mountains and forests surround the stones.

冶力关莲花峰

莲花峰为兴隆山的顶峰，海拔3300米，因酷似一朵莲花盛开在万顷绿波翠色之中而得名。莲花峰自然景观秀丽，境内地形地貌迥异，原始森林高山草甸相互辉映，浑然天成。

Lotus Mountain at Yeliguan Town

As high as 3300 meters, Lotus Mountain is so named because it looks like a lotus in bloom. The mountain is delicate and graceful with a variety of landforms, including virgin forests and alpine meadows.

风俗节庆
Customs and Festivals

> 玛尼石

　　玛尼石，泛指刻有玛尼字样或神佛形象的石块。玛尼是佛教经咒六字真言"唵、嘛、呢、叭、咪、吽"的简称，可谓"玛尼石"一词的由来。

Marnyi Stones

Marnyi Stones, generally refer to the stone blocks inscribed with Marnyi characters or images of gods and Buddha. Marnyi is an abbreviation for the scriptures Om Mani Padme Hum.

玛尼堆和风马旗

藏区随处可见大大小小的玛尼石堆，部分上面刻有六字真言、神像或各种吉祥图案，也有些不刻任何图案而仅仅是石板、石块叠堆而成。这是藏区人民祈福的一种方式。风马，藏语称隆达。"隆"即风，"达"即马。风马常被印刷成小方纸片以供法事或经过垭口时抛洒，有时也被印成旗帜连成一片悬挂在垭口、民居或寺庙上方。

Marnyi Stone Piles and Religious Flags

Marnyi stone piles of various sizes can be seen virtually everywhere in Tibet. On some of the stones there are inscriptions of Om Mani Padme Hum, images of gods or other significant patterns. There are also piles without any patterns, only stones. This is a way for Tibetans to pray for blessings.

煨桑

　　煨桑是藏区最古老、最普遍的一种民间祭祀活动，一般在夏季五六月举行。藏族人在松柏枝上加香料，点燃桑烟、遍撒龙达祈祷祝福。图为抛洒龙达的藏民。

Weisang

Weisang or "burning offerings for smoke" is the oldest and most popular sacrifice in Tibet. It usually happens in May or June.

添嘛呢箭杆的僧人

在藏族地区，几乎每家每户都备有桑炉（或者在院子中央，或者在屋顶依山处），每逢藏历新年大年初一，人们起床后第一件事就是煨桑祭神，素以第一个去煨桑的人为荣。后来的人只是在已经燃起的煨桑堆上加松枝、柏枝、桑面（糌粑）等物，顺便献酒洒浆，跪拜叩首，添嘛呢箭杆。

Weisang, Monks adding Mani arrow shafts

In Tibet, nearly every household has a mulberry furnace. On the first day of the new year in the Tibetan Calendar people get up early and the first thing they do is to burn offerings for smoke in worship ceremonies. The people coming later need only to add branches of pine and cypress or Sangmian (glutinous rice cakes) onto the burning piles. They will then offer liquors as well, kowtow on bended knees and add Mani arrow shafts.

磕长头（一）

藏传佛教信仰者最至诚的礼佛方式之一。磕头朝圣的人在其五体投地的时候，是为"身"敬；口中不断念咒，是为"语"敬；心中不断想着佛，是为"意"敬。"磕长头"分为长途、短途、就地三种形式。

Long-time Kowtows (1)

Long-time kowtows are one of the most sincere ways of worshiping Buddha by believers of Tibetan Buddhism. These behaviors include those for long and short distance, as well as those in the same place.

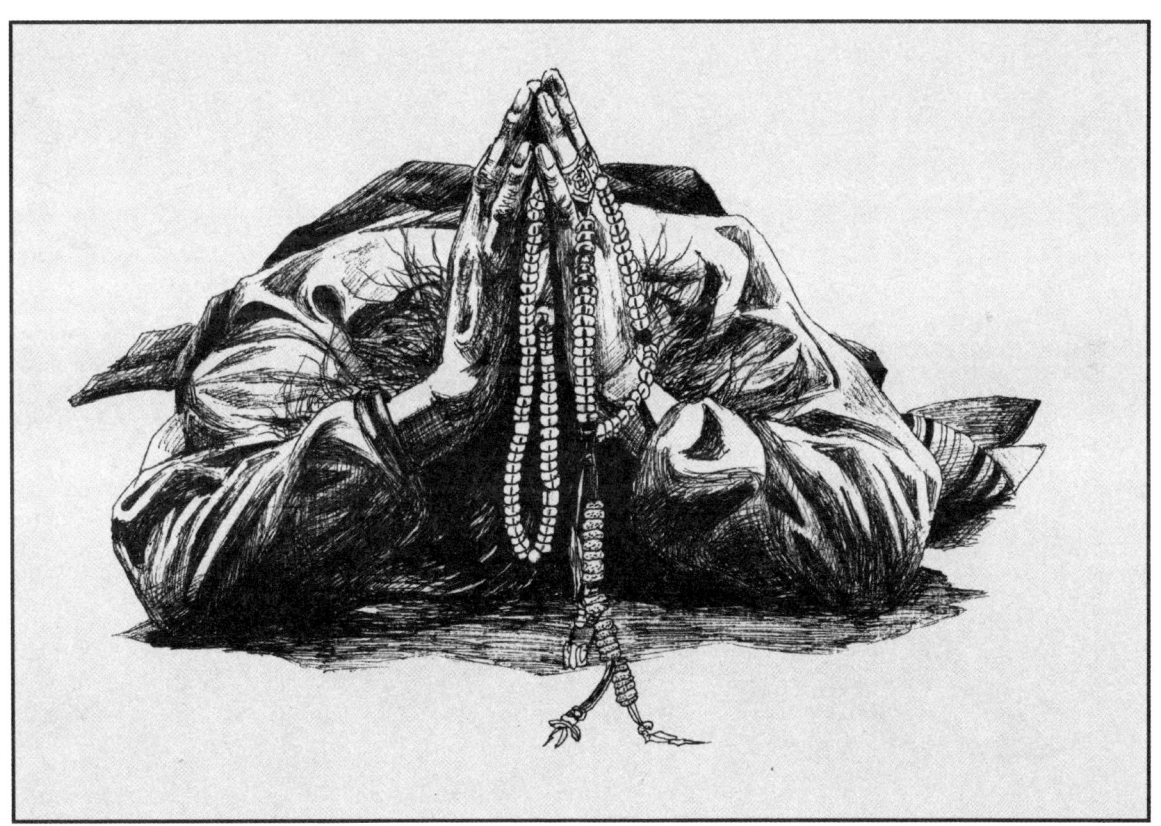

磕长头（二）

磕长头是藏传佛教盛行的地区，信徒们的一种虔诚的拜佛仪式。在各地通往拉萨的大道上，可以不时地见到信徒们从遥远的故乡开始，手戴护具、膝着护膝，前身挂一毛皮衣物，不惧辛苦，三步一磕，或积月、或积年而至目的地朝佛。相识的人们三五成队，在共同信念的支配下，虔诚地移步而行。

Long-time Kowtows (2)

Long-time kowtows are reverent exercises for worshiping Buddha by believers in the area where Tibetan Buddhism is popular. In the path to Lhasa from various places, believers can be seen occasionally kowtowing by walking from their hometowns, some of which are quite a distance from Lhasa. It may take months or even years for them in this way to show their respect for Buddha on their way to the capital city.

磕长头（三）

在甘南的任何一座寺院都可以见到就地磕长头的信徒，同一个地方，同一个动作，不断地重复，执着地表达着虔诚信仰。

Long-time Kowtows (3)

In every temple in Gannan visitors can see believers kowtowing again and again. In the same place, they repeat the same gesture one after another to show their piety.

寺院门前拜佛妇女

　　寺院门前妇女双手合十，恭敬地伏下身子，双手向前直伸，三步一磕，五体投地。藏族信徒以"磕长头"的方式虔诚的拜佛，每伏身一次，以手划地为号，起身后前行到记号处再匍匐，如此周而复始。

Women Worshiping Buddha in Front of a Temple

Women with a Zen gesture gets her body down to the ground with respect and both hands stretch straight forward. They practice kowtows every three steps with complete prostration because Tibetan believers show their reverent worship towards Buddha with these complex kowtows.

转转经筒的老人（一）

在甘南随处都能见到长长的转经廊，每天有无数的僧人和信众推动着转经筒，虔诚地祈祷。

Corridor of Prayer wheels (1)

In Gannan, long corridors for prayer wheels can be seen nearly everywhere. Countless monks and believers turn the prayer wheels there in their sincere prayer.

转经筒的老人（二）

在甘南几乎所有老人的手中都有一个小转经筒，这种手摇转经筒又叫作"手摇玛尼轮"，质地有金、银、铜等，也分大、中、小几种。转经筒内装着"六字大明咒"经卷，每摇一圈就等于念诵经文一遍。藏传佛教认为，持诵六字真言越多，表示对佛对菩萨越虔诚，由此可得脱离轮回之苦。

Corridor of Prayer Wheels (2)

In Gannan, nearly every old person holds a small prayer wheel upon which there is the text of Om Mani Pedme Hong. For every round of the wheel, the prayer chants the text once over.

晒佛节

每年正月的法会是甘南藏传佛教法会中最为盛大的佛教法会。信众聚集，场面尤为壮观。届时会有巨幅的佛像唐卡在晒佛台展出。

Shaifo Festival

In January of the Tibetan Calendar, a dharma assembly of the largest scale in Tibetan Buddhism takes place in Gannan. On those occasions, a huge thangka (a kind of religious drawing) of Buddha will be exhibited.

晒佛节的巨型佛像

每年正月十三的晒佛节是甘南一年中规模最大、最为隆重的宗教节日,届时会展出巨大的佛像,供来自世界各地的数万僧众信徒瞻仰。

Huge Buddha Statue in Shaifo Festival

Taking place on January 13th of Tibetan Calendar every year, the festival is the holy day with a grand ceremony of the largest scale. On that occasion, a huge statue of Buddha will be exhibited for monks and believers from all over the world to visit with reverence.

法舞

法舞，学名为"金刚驱魔神舞"。它是在西藏土风舞的基础上，吸取了藏传佛教仪规和印度瑜伽宗面具舞的某些形式，而形成的一种藏传佛教密乘仪式舞蹈。法舞有独特的面具、服饰、乐曲和舞蹈程式，音乐抑扬顿挫，舞姿酣畅淋漓，富有极强的震撼力。它把民间传统的驱祟避邪与祈祷人寿康泰相结合，具有深厚的文化内涵。

Ceremonial Dances

ICeremonial dances for Tibetan Buddhism were developed on the basis of Tibetan country-dance, absorbing some performing forms of Tibetan Buddhism and the mask dancing of yeshiva. Featuring unique masks, costumes, and music in addition to dancing with lively rhythms, the ceremonial dances are very touching. They combine driving and avoiding evil spirits with praying for longevity in health with profound cultural meanings.

> 法舞面具

　　跳法舞时所带的面具是仿照其所代表的密宗神像的面部而制作的，有金刚、护法、僧人、恶鬼等，表达了角色内容和丰富的宗教文化内涵。法舞面具是一种象征符号，是法舞表演不可缺少的道具。

Masks of Ceremonial Dances

These masks represent the faces of the gods in Vajrayana. They show the characters of the gods with religious and cultural meanings. The masks are symbolic signs, indispensable properties in the ceremonial dances.

法舞鹿神舞

鹿神舞是由僧人头戴鹿和牦牛面具的舞蹈,以鹿、牛等动物住空旷荒野而喻诸法之空相。自古以来,在藏族人民的心中鹿是安宁、自由的象征,藏族人民往往把美好的愿望都寄托于鹿的身上。

Deer-God Dancing, Ceremonial Dance

Monks are depicted dancing with the masks of the deer god and yak god. Since ancient times, Tibetans believe that deer are the symbol of peace and freedom. Therefore, they often put their best wishes on these audacious animals.

法舞大合舞

大合舞是法舞中一段众人共同表演的舞蹈，由头带面具饰仆从者拥簇一个"大施主"的角色入场。"大施主"所带面具是一个汉僧的笑脸，后面跟着几位黄面及青面的天界勇士，互相耳语打闹，逗人发笑。大合舞表示成佛后带领众生得乐。

Mass Dancing, Ceremonial Dances

Mass dancing is a piece of dance performed by a group of people. The group is led by the character of "generous donor" who is clustered around by attendants with masks. The generous donor wears the mask of a smiling Chinese monk followed by several heavenly warriors with yellow or blue faces.

声乐僧

声乐僧是在举行法会时，专门负责乐器演奏的僧人。演奏的乐器有鼓、钦、铃、铜号、铙钹、筚篥、骨号等。

Music Monks

Music monks play many types of instruments including drums, Qin, bells, brass trumpets, cymbals, hichiriki, and born trumpets in dharma assemblies.

吹藏号的声乐僧

僧人所演奏的藏号，由紫铜和黄铜制成，雕刻精美，有大、中、小等型号，是最为常见的伴奏乐器。

Monks blowing Tibetan Trombones

Tibetan trombones are made from red copper and brass, with delicate carvings. They are the most common instruments for acoompaniment that are divided into large, medium and small sizes.

酥油花灯节（一）

藏历正月十五这天，藏民族居住的地方多会摆出用五彩酥油雕塑成的花鸟鱼虫和人物形象，欢庆酥油花灯节。甘南各地的僧俗民众以及民间艺术家们用本地盛产的酥油和颜料，制作出精致的酥油花，许多酥油花还以多个画幅构成连环故事，讲述藏民族的古老传说。

Ghee Lantern Festival (1)

On January 15th of the Tibetan calendar, Tibetans usually make lanterns in the shapes of flowers, birds, fish, insects and humans made of full, colorful ghee to celebrate the Ghee Lantern Festival. They are hand-made by monks, followers and folk artists in nearly every corner of Gannan from the abundant ghee found in this region. They are delicate and often tell age-old legends in Tibet by joining the images on them into a series of stories.

酥油花灯节（二）

为了雕刻花灯，僧人们在大冬天里要不时将手放进刺骨的冰水中降温，用冰冷的手迅速拿取酥油在扎好的骨架上塑形，最后安装在高大的木架上供人参观。

Ghee Lantern Festival (2)

To engrave the lanterns in winter, monks frequently need to put their hands into icy water to cool them so that they can pick ghee and put it on the framework to make figures on the lanterns. Finally, the lanterns are placed on tall wooden stands for visiting.

[酥油佛像花灯]

酥油花是藏传佛教艺术雕塑的一种特殊形式,以酥油为原料,以佛教人物、花卉、飞禽、走兽、树木等为题材,造型精巧、形象逼真,是令人叹为观止的精美艺术品。

Buddha Statue Lantern Made of Ghee

Ghee lanterns demonstrate a special kind of artistic sculpture in Tibetan Buddhism. They are made into the shapes of Buddhist figures, flowers, birds, beasts, trees and other natural wonders. They are exquisite, vivid and unique forms of art.

格萨尔摔跤

格萨尔摔跤是一种历史悠久，流行于藏族地区的体育竞技运动。摔跤手裸露着上身，背涂酥油，下身穿半截短裤，腰束布带，足蹬藏靴做交臂、拉腰、绊足等动作。

Gesar Wrestling

Tibetan Wrestling is an athletic sport popular in this populated region of Tibet. Wrestlers appear with their naked upper body smeared with ghee, short pants and Tibetan boots in addition to a cotton tape around their waist. They wrestle with their arms, pull waists and grapple with each other.

> 格萨尔赛马

　　赛马是藏族民众十分喜爱的一项活动，它不仅是牧民闲暇之余交流农牧业生产经验的场所，而且是藏民族精神的展示。格萨尔赛马大会一般会在每年农历的八月十三日开始，持续七天左右。

Gesar Horse Racing

Horse racing is an activity loved by Tibetans. It is an opportunity for herders to meet each other, exchange experience on agriculture and animal husbandry, and showcase the spirit of Tibetans. Gesar Horse racing takes place on August 13th each year.

赛马骑手

赛马大会是年轻小伙展示男子气概的好机会,若在比赛中拔得头筹,那么在藏区可谓是极大的荣誉。赛马充分体现了草原汉子的野性之美,同时也是姑娘们寻找意中人的理想之地。

Horse Racers

Horse racing is a good opportunity for young men to show their masculinity as it demonstrates the beauty and savagery of those raised on the grassland. It is also an ideal place for girls to find their "Mr. Right."

[赛牦牛]

　　赛牦牛是藏族传统特色的体育项目，由经验丰富的牧民驾驭性情暴躁的牦牛进行赛跑比赛。比赛时，牧民骑手待于起跑线，发令后即纵马狂奔，以先到终点为胜。获胜者会受到观众的热烈祝贺并得到酒肉奖励。

Yak Racing

Yak racing is a traditional sport in which experienced herders compete with each other by riding yaks. The winners will be congratulated by the spectators and presented with awards of wine and meat.

| 香浪节舞蹈 |

　　香浪节是中国西部草原上最热烈的狂欢节，是精彩绝伦的草原盛会。此节日源于拉卜楞寺僧人每年外出采集木柴的活动，后逐渐演变成僧俗一同郊游的节日。"香浪"在藏语中有"采薪"之意，因藏语称木柴为"香"，樵采称"浪"，故名"香浪"。香浪节上牧民穿着艳丽的华服，惊艳美貌的藏族姑娘跳起欢快的藏舞，气氛欢快热烈。

Dancing during Xianglang Festival

Xianglang Festival is the busiest Carnival on the grassland in western China and features games that have a strong local flavor. This festival originated from the Labrang Monastery in which monks went out to pick up firewood. Such an activity was developed into a festival when monks and others enjoyed the excursion.

香浪节马队表演

香浪节是甘南藏族自治州的民俗节日。在欢度节日期间，人们以村寨为单位，在美酒、乳酪、奶茶的相伴下度过十天半月的野外生活。在过节时开展村与村，家庭与家庭之间的赛马、拔河等娱乐游戏。

Horse-racing during the Xianglang Festival

During Xianglang Festival, a traditional, non-official festive day in Gannan, the people of villages of three to five households get together and race horses. They also compete at tug-of-wars and other recreational games that are organized between households or villages.

博峪采花节

　　博峪采花节是甘肃省舟曲县博峪乡藏族群众的传统节庆活动,又叫"女儿节",为期二天,于每年农历五月初五举行。它大致由"抢水"、"采花"、"祝福"三个部分构成,载歌载舞,欢庆异常。

Boyu Flower-picking Festival

A traditional festival also known as "The Festival of Girls", it is celebrated by Tibetans in Boyu Township of Zhouqu County in Gansu Province. It is divided into three parts including water grabbing, flower picking and praying combined with festive singing and dancing.

绘制坛城的小阿卡（一）

坛城源于印度佛教密宗，系密宗本尊及眷属聚集的道场，是藏传佛教密宗修行时必须供奉的一种对象。坛城作为象征宇宙世界结构的本源，是变化多样的本尊神及眷属众神聚居处的模型缩影。全手工绘制的坛城精美无比，而在法会结束时僧人会将辛苦绘制的图案尽数抹掉，以示"一切有为法，如梦幻泡沫"的佛家思想。

Painting Sand Mandala (1)

Sand Mandala was originated from Vajrayana. It was an object the followers of this school must enshrine and worship. The delicate Sand Mandala was made entirely by hand. After each dharma assembly, Buddhist monks will erase the hand-made drawings to demonstrate the Buddhist idea that everything physical will disappear, like dreams, one day or another.

绘制坛城的小阿卡（二）

　　从 2500 多年前佛陀亲自教导弟子制作沙坛城开始，这门精致绝伦的宗教艺术，就历代相承、毫无间断。

Painting Sand Mandala (2)

2500 years ago, Buddha began to teach his followers how to make Sand Mandala. This refined religious art has been carried on through dynasties.

绘制唐卡

唐卡画师在绘制唐卡前，首先要卜吉日、焚香祷告，然后边诵经边备料。备料包括绘画所用的画布和颜料，画布选用的是平滑棉布，上面不能有任何污点、小孔或裂缝。

Painting thangkas

Before the painting of thangkas, painters need to foretell and select an auspicious day. Then he or she will burn incense and pray, making preparation while chanting sutras. They prepare canvases and pigments. The canvases must be smooth cotton fabric without any stains, pinholes or fissures.

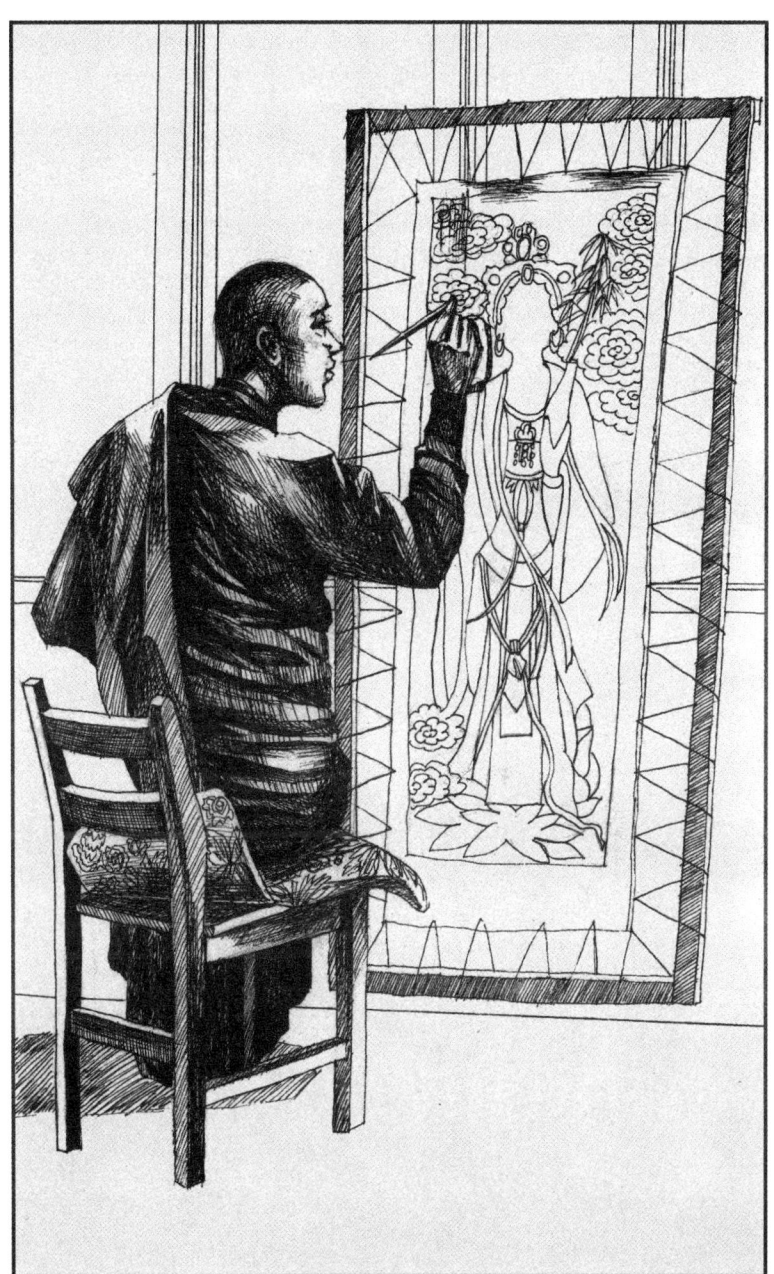

上师为弟子加持

上师是藏佛教对具有高德胜行，堪为世人表率者之尊称，又叫"喇嘛"。上师的加持分"身"、"语"、"意"三个方面，通过上师的加持，使弟子的心和佛心融为一体，提升智慧。

A Guru Enchanting His Followers

A Guru is a monk with good behavior and morality who is followed and respected by believers in Tibetan Buddhism. He is also called Lama. The enchantment is delivered through bodies, minds and language. Through this process, the master helps his followers to integrate their minds with Buddhism.

喇嘛向众人施与圣水

寺院的喇嘛向前来寺院参拜的人们分发寺院圣水，人们纷纷争抢，希望得到神佛的保佑。

Lamas Distributing Holy Water to the Public

Lamas are distributing holy water to the followers that are visiting their temple. The receivers are scrambling for the water. They desire the blessing and the protection from gods and Buddha.

护法僧

护法僧是在寺院举行法会时，身着盛装，手拿木棒、铁棒等，维护秩序的僧人。

Custodian Monks

Custodian monks are those who maintain order during dharma assemblies in splendid attire with wood or iron bars in their hands.

> 练习法舞

学习法舞的僧人在平时要苦练基本功。关于法舞的动作,有严格的要求。比如,上身犹如狮子,肌肉要放松,举止应尊严,作舞亦缓慢,膝盖要弯曲,骨骼现安乐等等。

Practicing Ceremonial Dances

The Buddhist monks learning ceremonial dances need to diligently practice the basic skills. There are strict requirements for the movements of ceremonial dances.

亮宝

每逢藏历二月八日，僧人要衣着整齐，手持平常不取出示人的法器宝物，随着仪仗队绕寺一周。

Showing Treasures
On February 8th every year, monks appear in tidy dress holding musical instruments or other rarely shown treasures while walking around their temple following honor guards.

喇嘛辩经

辩经是佛教用语，是对佛教理论的辩论，即僧人为了加强对佛经的真正理解，采用一问一答的方式交流所学心得和所悟佛法，如同学术讨论一般。辩经的起势是拍手，右手高高举起，用力一拍左手，一个炸雷般的拍手声便响在了坐着的喇嘛头上或额前。拍手有两个作用：一是表示我现在向你提问，请你赶快回答并致敬；一是表示在气势上要威慑对手。

Debating on Buddhist scriptures by Lamas

In debating, Buddhist monks answer each question on Buddhist texts or theories successively and exchange their opinions to further their understanding of Buddhism. The clapping of hands has two functions: 1) to show that I am asking you questions that you need to answer in order to show your respect to me and 2) to deter my opponent by behaving aggressively.

吃早饭的僧侣

寺院中的僧侣每天严格按照作息时间活动,统一时间吃饭、上课。僧侣们在寺院里过着紧张忙碌的学习生活,一刻也不敢懈怠。

Monks Eating Breakfast

Monks follow strict timetables for work and rest, including eating and going to class together at specific times. They are diligent in their studies and cultivation of themselves.

> 献哈达

　　"献哈达"是藏族人民最普遍的一种礼节。每逢婚丧节庆、迎来送往、拜会尊长、觐见佛像、送别远行等,都有献哈达的习惯。献哈达是对对方表示纯洁、忠诚、尊敬的意思。"哈达"是一种生丝织品,纺得稀松如网,也有用丝绸为料的。

Presenting Khatag

Presenting a Khatag, a piece of silk, to guests is one of the most popular forms of etiquette in this Tibetan region. It symbolizes an immaculacy, sincerity, loyalty and respect toward the guests.

藏粑

　　藏粑是甘南藏族群众日常食用的主食之一，它是用大麦炒熟后制作的。吃法是先用砖茶烧一锅茶，放入适量的盐，再放入酥油打成酥油茶，然后用酥油茶拌炒面，用手抓着吃。

Zangba

Zangba is a staple food for the Tibetan people in Gannan. It consists mainly of stir-fried barley. When eaten it is generally accompanied by buttered tea, made by adding salt and ghee to a pot of brick tea. Then the fried barley powder is mixed into the buttered tea, blended together and eaten with bare hands.

| 牛背上的孩子 |

在甘南许多地方，人们依然保持着以马匹、牦牛为主要交通工具的传统出行方式，体现出人与动物、环境和谐共处的自然风貌。

Children on the Back of Yak

In many places of Gannan horses and yaks, main vehicles in the past, are still used by people for travel. With this means of transportation, humans and animals live in harmony with the environment. It makes for a beautiful and natural landscape!

甘南藏族妇女服饰

长袍是甘南藏族妇女春夏秋冬必穿的衣服，偏右开襟，以腰带系之，其面料多用毛哗叽、黑华呢等。夏季夹里为布料或丝绸，冬季夹里为白羔皮。衣边缝缀二至四寸宽的水獭皮，装饰珊瑚、金银、各类宝石，富丽华贵，色彩缤纷。

Dresses of Tibetan Women in Gannan

These robes are examples of the clothes Tibetan women in Gannan usually wear in all seasons. They features buttons on the right side and a waistband.

藏獒

藏獒是在高寒生态环境中生活的珍贵犬种，体形高大、性情凶猛，可以抗击野兽，是牧民不可或缺的忠实伙伴。

Tibetan Mastiff

Tall, fierce and strong enough to fight off wild animals, the Tibetan mastiff in Hequ is an indispensible and loyal friend to local herders.

巡街仪式中的羊

在法会正式开始之前，先要举行巡街仪式，有华丽的仪仗队、乐队，还有吉祥物，如洁白的羊或牦牛等。

Sheep on Parade

Before a dharma assembly there is a parade with an honor guard and a band in shining uniforms. They are often joined by pure white sheep, yaks and other mascots.